ADVANCED
PYTHON

UPSCALE YOUR PROGRAMMING EXPERTISE & BUILD AWESOME APPS

KARTHIK MANI

https://www.linkedin.com/in/softwarekarthik/

FOREWORD

I am Karthik, the author of this book who has years of experience with Python. I have started my career as a web designer and now I have grown as a full-stack developer. Python has always been my favourite and wonderful tool to build dynamic websites, data manipulations and automation processes.

Python is versatile, you can build a web application, you can analyse your data and you can automate your workflows.

Even an advanced-level programmer doesn't follow any good practices in Python, truly they don't know. For professional developers who want to make their Python code in a good manner, I wrote this book with all essential advanced topics. If you are a beginner, intermediate, or advanced-level programmer, this book is very useful to all. I will update this book whenever new topics arise in the Python world.

Happy Coding!

- Karthik Mani

Table of Contents

Introduction

Python is a versatile and powerful programming language that offers a wide range of advanced topics and features. Here are some advanced topics in Python:

1. **Decorators:** Decorators allow you to modify or enhance the behavior of functions or methods. They are widely used for tasks like logging, authentication, and measuring execution time.

2. **Generators and Iterators:** Python supports the creation of iterators and generators, which enable you to work with large datasets efficiently and lazily, without loading everything into memory at once.

3. **Context Managers:** Context managers are used to efficiently manage resources, such as files, database connections, and network sockets, by using the `with` statement.

4. **Metaclasses:** Metaclasses allow you to define the behavior and structure of classes, making it possible to customize class creation and object initialization.

5. **Multiple Inheritance:** Python supports multiple inheritance, allowing a class to inherit attributes and methods from more than one base class. Understanding and using multiple inheritance effectively is an advanced topic.

6. Dynamic Typing and Duck Typing: Python is dynamically typed, which means variable types are determined at runtime. Understanding how Python handles data types and using duck typing is crucial.

7. Magic Methods (Dunder Methods): Python has a set of special methods that start and end with double underscores *(e.g., `__init__`, `__str__`)*. These methods allow you to define custom behavior for your objects.

8. Closures and Function Scoping: Closures are functions that remember the environment in which they were created. Understanding scoping rules is essential for working with closures effectively.

9. Asynchronous Programming: Python supports asynchronous programming using the `async` and `await` keywords, allowing you to write non-blocking code for tasks like web scraping and network operations.

10. Multithreading and Multiprocessing: Python provides modules like `threading` and `multiprocessing` for concurrent programming. This is important for tasks that require parallelism to utilize multiple CPU cores.

11. Regular Expressions: Python's `re` module allows you to work with regular expressions, which are powerful for text processing and pattern matching.

12. Python Standard Library Modules: There are many advanced modules in the Python Standard Library, including `collections`, `itertools`, `functools`, and `datetime`, which provide advanced data manipulation and time handling capabilities.

13. NumPy and SciPy: These libraries are widely used for scientific computing, offering support for large, multi-dimensional arrays and mathematical functions.

14. Data Serialization: Understanding how to serialize data using formats like JSON, XML, and binary formats, and using libraries like `pickle`, is crucial for data storage and interchange.

15. Cython and Numba: These tools allow you to write Python code that can be compiled to C for performance optimization, especially in computationally intensive applications.

16. Web Frameworks: If you're interested in web development, advanced knowledge of web frameworks like Django and Flask is essential.

17. Machine Learning and Data Science Libraries: Python is widely used in the fields of machine learning and data science, with libraries like scikit-learn, TensorFlow, and PyTorch.

18. GUI Development: You can create graphical user interfaces using libraries like Tkinter, PyQt, and Kivy.

19. Custom Module and Package Development:
Learning how to create your own modules and
packages is essential for building large-scale
Python applications.

20. Debugging and Profiling: Understanding
advanced debugging and profiling tools like
`pdb`, `cProfile`, and `line_profiler` can help
identify and fix performance issues in your code.

These advanced topics in Python can take your
programming skills to the next level and allow you
to tackle a wide range of complex tasks and
projects. Depending on your specific interests and
needs, you may choose to delve deeper into one or
more of these areas.

Python Decorators

In Python, decorators are a powerful and flexible way to modify or <u>extend the behavior of functions</u> or methods.

Decorators allow you to wrap a function with additional functionality without modifying its code directly. They are often used for tasks such as logging, caching, access control, and more.

Here's an explanation of decorators along with some examples:

Basic Decorator:

A basic decorator is a function that takes another function as an argument, adds some functionality, and returns a new function. The `@decorator` syntax is a convenient way to apply decorators to functions.

```
def my_decorator(func):

    def wrapper():

        print("Something is happening before the function
is called.")

        func()

        print("Something is happening after the function is
called.")

    return wrapper


@my_decorator
def say_hello():

    print("Hello!")


say_hello()
```

In this example, `my_decorator` is a decorator that wraps the `say_hello` function. When `say_hello` is called, it's actually the `wrapper` function inside `my_decorator` that gets executed, adding extra functionality.

Decorators with Arguments:

You can create decorators that take arguments for added flexibility. Here's an example:

```python
def repeat(n):
    def decorator(func):
        def wrapper(*args, kwargs):
            for _ in range(n):
                func(*args, kwargs)
        return wrapper
    return decorator


@repeat(3)
def say_hello():
    print("Hello!")


say_hello()
```

In this example, the `repeat` decorator takes an argument `n` and returns a decorator function. The returned decorator is then applied to the `say_hello` function, causing it to be executed three times.

Class-Based Decorators:

Decorators can also be implemented using classes. The class must implement the `__call__` method.

```python
class MyDecorator:
    def __init__(self, func):
        self.func = func

    def __call__(self, *args, kwargs):
        print("Something is happening before the function is called.")
        self.func(*args, kwargs)
        print("Something is happening after the function is called.")
```

```
@MyDecorator
def say_hello():
  print("Hello!")


say_hello()
```

Practical Example: Logging Decorator

A common use case for decorators is logging.

Here's a simple logging decorator:

```
def log_function_call(func):
  def wrapper(*args, kwargs):
    print(f"Calling {func.__name__} with args:
{args}, kwargs: {kwargs}")
    result = func(*args, kwargs)
    print(f"{func.__name__} returned: {result}")
    return result
  return wrapper
```

```
@log_function_call
def add(x, y):
    return x + y


result = add(3, 5)
```

In this example, the `log_function_call` decorator logs information about the function call, including its name, arguments, and return value.

Decorators are a powerful tool in Python, and they provide a clean and concise way to extend the behavior of functions or methods. They are widely used in frameworks like Flask and Django for tasks such as routing and authentication.

Generators & Iterators

Generators and iterators are concepts in Python that facilitate efficient and memory-friendly processing of large datasets. They allow you to work with sequences of data without loading the entire sequence into memory at once.

Iterators:

An iterator is an object that can be iterated (looped) over. In Python, an iterator must implement two methods: `__iter__()` and `__next__()`.

- `__iter__()` returns the iterator object itself.

- `__next__()` returns the next value from the iterator. When there are no more items to return, it should raise `StopIteration`.

Here's a simple example of an iterator:

```python
class MyIterator:
    def __init__(self, start, end):
        self.current = start
        self.end = end


    def __iter__(self):
        return self


    def __next__(self):
        if self.current >= self.end:
            raise StopIteration
        else:
            self.current += 1
            return self.current - 1


# Usage:
my_iterator = MyIterator(1, 5)
for num in my_iterator:
    print(num)
```

Generators:

Generators are a concise way to create iterators in Python. They use the `yield` keyword to produce a series of values lazily. The generator function is paused after each `yield` statement, and the state is retained, allowing the function to resume from where it left off.

Here's an example of a simple generator function:

```python
def simple_generator(start, end):
    current = start
    while current < end:
        yield current
        current += 1

# Usage:
my_generator = simple_generator(1, 5)
for num in my_generator:
    print(num)
```

In this example, `simple_generator` is a generator function that produces numbers from `start` to `end`. The `yield` statement is used to emit each value, and the generator retains its state between calls.

Advantages of Generators:

1. Memory Efficiency:

Generators generate values one at a time and don't store the entire sequence in memory, making them memory-efficient for large datasets.

2. Lazy Evaluation:

Values are generated on-demand, which allows for lazy evaluation. This is particularly useful when dealing with infinite sequences or large datasets.

3. Easier to Read and Write:

Generator functions are often more concise and easier to read than equivalent iterator classes.

4. State Retention:

Generators automatically retain their state between calls, making it easy to write code that maintains context between iterations.

Generator Expressions:

In addition to using `yield` in a function, you can create generator expressions, which are similar to list comprehensions but use parentheses instead of square brackets. Generator expressions are particularly useful when you need a simple one-time generator.

```
# Generator expression
my_generator = (x for x in range(1, 5))


# Usage:
for num in my_generator:
    print(num)
```

Generators and iterators are powerful tools in Python for handling large datasets and performing lazy evaluation, contributing to more memory-efficient and readable code.

Context managers in Python provide a convenient way to manage resources, such as files, network connections, or database connections, by defining setup and teardown actions. They ensure that resources are acquired and released properly, even in the presence of exceptions. Context managers are commonly used with the `with` statement.

There are two ways to implement a context manager in Python:

1. Using Classes with `__enter__` and `__exit__` Methods:

You can create a class with `__enter__` and `__exit__` methods to define the setup and teardown actions.

```python
class MyContextManager:
    def __enter__(self):
        print("Entering the context")
        # Setup actions, resource acquisition, etc.
        return self  # Return the resource to be managed

    def __exit__(self, exc_type, exc_value, traceback):
        print("Exiting the context")
        # Teardown actions, resource release, etc.
        # Optional: Handle exceptions if needed
        return False  # If False, exceptions will propagate; if True, exceptions will be suppressed
```

```
# Usage:

with MyContextManager() as cm:

    print("Inside the context")

    # Resource is acquired and managed here


# Upon exiting the block, the context manager's
__exit__ method is called
```

2. Using the `contextlib` Module and `contextmanager` Decorator:

The `contextlib` module provides the `contextmanager` decorator, allowing you to define a context manager using a generator function with the `yield` statement.

```
from contextlib import contextmanager


@contextmanager
def my_context_manager():

    print("Entering the context")

    # Setup actions, resource acquisition, etc.
```

```python
    yield   # This is where the block of code inside the
'with' statement is executed

    print("Exiting the context")

    # Teardown actions, resource release, etc.


# Usage:

with my_context_manager():

    print("Inside the context")

    # Resource is acquired and managed here


# Upon exiting the block, the context manager's
teardown actions are performed
```

Example: File Handling with Context Manager

Here's an example using a context manager to handle file operations:

```python
# Using Class-based Context Manager
class FileHandler:
    def __init__(self, filename, mode):
        self.filename = filename
        self.mode = mode

    def __enter__(self):
        self.file = open(self.filename, self.mode)
        return self.file

    def __exit__(self, exc_type, exc_value, traceback):
        self.file.close()

# Usage:
with FileHandler('example.txt', 'w') as file:
    file.write('Hello, Context Manager!')
```

```python
# Using @contextmanager Decorator

from contextlib import contextmanager


@contextmanager
def file_handler(filename, mode):
    file = open(filename, mode)
    yield file
    file.close()


# Usage:
with file_handler('example.txt', 'r') as file:
    content = file.read()
    print(content)
```

In both cases, the context manager ensures that the file is properly closed, even if an exception occurs within the `with` block. Context managers are useful for managing resources and improving the readability of your code.

Metaclasses

Metaclasses are a powerful yet advanced feature in Python that allow you to customize the creation and behavior of classes. A metaclass is a class of a class, defining how a class behaves. Metaclasses are often used for code introspection, code injection, and enforcing coding conventions.

In Python, everything is an object, including classes. When you define a class, it is an instance of a metaclass. By default, the metaclass is the built-in `type`. However, you can create your own metaclasses to modify the behavior of class creation.

Here's a simple example to illustrate the concept of metaclasses:

```python
# Custom metaclass
class MyMeta(type):
    def __new__(cls, name, bases, attrs):
        # Modify attributes or do additional processing here
        attrs['modified_attribute'] = 42
        return super().__new__(cls, name, bases, attrs)


# Using the custom metaclass
class MyClass(metaclass=MyMeta):
    original_attribute = 10


# Instances of the class will have the modified_attribute
obj = MyClass()
print(obj.modified_attribute)  # Outputs: 42
```

In this example, `MyMeta` is a custom metaclass that subclasses `type`. The `__new__` method is called when the class `MyClass` is created. In this method, you can modify the attributes of the class before it is created. In this case, we added a new attribute called `modified_attribute`.

Realtime Example:

Let's consider a more practical example where we use a metaclass to enforce a coding convention, such as making sure all method names start with "my_":

```
class ConventionMeta(type):
    def __new__(cls, name, bases, attrs):
        # Check method names and modify if needed
        for attr_name, attr_value in attrs.items():
```

```python
        if callable(attr_value) and
attr_name.startswith('my_'):

            print(f"Method name {attr_name} follows
the convention.")

        elif callable(attr_value):

            new_name = f"my_{attr_name}"

            print(f"Renaming method {attr_name} to
{new_name}.")

            attrs[new_name] = attrs.pop(attr_name)


    return super().__new__(cls, name, bases, attrs)


# Using the metaclass to enforce the convention
class
MyClassWithConvention(metaclass=ConventionMe
ta):
  def my_method(self):
    pass


  def another_method(self):
    pass
```

In this example, the `ConventionMeta` metaclass checks the method names of the class and ensures that they follow the convention of starting with "my_". If a method does not follow the convention, it is renamed accordingly.

Metaclasses are a powerful tool, but they should be used judiciously as they can make code less readable and more complex. They are often unnecessary for most applications, and simpler solutions, such as decorators or class inheritance, might be more appropriate.

Multiple Inheritance

Multiple inheritance in Python refers to the ability of a class to inherit attributes and methods from more than one parent class. While Python supports multiple inheritance, it's important to use it carefully to avoid potential issues like the diamond problem. The diamond problem occurs when a class inherits from two classes that have a common ancestor, leading to ambiguity in method resolution.

Here's a simple example to illustrate multiple inheritance:

```
class Animal:
    def speak(self):
        pass
```

```
class Mammal(Animal):

    def give_birth(self):

        pass


class Bird(Animal):

    def lay_eggs(self):

        pass


class Platypus(Mammal, Bird):

    pass


# Usage:

platypus = Platypus()

platypus.speak()     # Inherits from Animal

platypus.give_birth()  # Inherits from Mammal

platypus.lay_eggs()    # Inherits from Bird
```

In this example, we have an `Animal` class with a `speak` method, and two subclasses `Mammal` and `Bird`, each with additional methods. The

ADVANCED PYTHON

`Platypus` class then inherits from both `Mammal` and `Bird`, exhibiting multiple inheritance.

Method Resolution Order (MRO):

Python uses a method resolution order (MRO) to determine the order in which base classes are searched when a method is called on an object. The `__mro__` attribute or the `mro()` method of a class can be used to see the method resolution order.

```
print(Platypus.__mro__)
# Outputs: (<class '__main__.Platypus'>, <class '__main__.Mammal'>, <class '__main__.Bird'>, <class '__main__.Animal'>, <class 'object'>)
```

In the example, the MRO for `Platypus` is `(Platypus, Mammal, Bird, Animal, object)`, meaning that method resolution will start with `Platypus`, then go to `Mammal`, followed by `Bird`, `Animal`, and finally, the base class `object`.

The Diamond Problem:

The diamond problem is a common issue in multiple inheritance when there is ambiguity about which version of a method to call. Consider the following example:

```python
class A:
    def method(self):
        print("A method")

class B(A):
    def method(self):
        print("B method")
```

```python
class C(A):
    def method(self):
        print("C method")


class D(B, C):
    pass


# Usage:
obj = D()
obj.method()
```

In this case, class `D` inherits from both `B` and `C`, which in turn inherit from `A`. When `D` calls `method()`, there is ambiguity because it could either call the version from `B` or from `C`. This ambiguity is the diamond problem.

To resolve the diamond problem, Python uses the C3 linearization algorithm, which defines a consistent and predictable order for method resolution.

In practice, it's often recommended to use multiple inheritance cautiously, favoring composition or other design patterns when possible to avoid potential issues and improve code maintainability.

Dynamic Typing & Duck Typing

Dynamic typing and duck typing are key concepts in Python that contribute to its flexibility and ease of use.

Dynamic Typing:

Dynamic typing means that the type of a variable is determined at runtime, rather than being explicitly declared at compile time.

In Python, you can assign values of any type to a variable, and the interpreter will dynamically determine the type during execution.

Here's an example of dynamic typing:

```python
x = 5  # x is an integer
print(type(x))  # Outputs: <class 'int'>

x = "Hello"  # x is now a string
print(type(x))  # Outputs: <class 'str'>
```

In this example, the variable `x` starts as an integer but is later assigned a string value. The type of `x` is dynamically determined based on the assigned value.

Duck Typing:

Duck typing is a programming concept that focuses on the behavior of an object rather than its type. The idea is that if an object walks like a duck and quacks like a duck, then it is a duck. In Python, this means that you can use an object based on its behavior (methods it has) rather than its explicit type.

Here's an example of duck typing:

```
class Dog:
    def speak(self):
        return "Woof!"

class Cat:
    def speak(self):
        return "Meow!"
```

```
class Duck:
    def speak(self):
        return "Quack!"


def animal_sound(animal):
    return animal.speak()


# Usage:
dog = Dog()
cat = Cat()
duck = Duck()


print(animal_sound(dog))  # Outputs: Woof!
print(animal_sound(cat))  # Outputs: Meow!
print(animal_sound(duck))  # Outputs: Quack!
```

In this example, the `animal_sound` function takes an argument `animal` and calls its `speak` method. The function doesn't care about the explicit type of the object; it just relies on the presence of the `speak` method.

Duck typing is often associated with the Pythonic philosophy of "Easier to ask for forgiveness than permission" (EAFP). This means that it's often better to try to use an object and handle any exceptions that may occur (if it doesn't have the expected method) rather than checking the type explicitly before using it.

```python
def animal_sound(animal):
    try:
        return animal.speak()
    except AttributeError:
        return "Unknown sound"


# Usage:
print(animal_sound(dog))  # Outputs: Woof!
print(animal_sound("Not an animal"))  # Outputs: Unknown sound
```

This approach allows for more flexible and generic code, making it easier to work with a variety of objects that share similar behaviors, even if they are of different types.

Magic Methods

Magic methods in Python, also known as dunder methods (double underscores), are special methods that start and end with double underscores.

These methods provide a way for classes to define specific behavior that gets invoked by the interpreter in response to certain operations. Magic methods enable operator overloading, customization of class behavior, and integration with built-in language features.

Here are some commonly used magic methods with examples:

`__init__`:

The `__init__` method is called when an object is created. It initializes the object's attributes.

```
class MyClass:
    def __init__(self, name):
        self.name = name


# Usage:
obj = MyClass("John")
print(obj.name)  # Outputs: John
```

`__str__` and `__repr__`:

The `__str__` method is called by the built-in `str()` function and `print()` to convert an object to a string. The `__repr__` method provides a string representation for debugging.

```
class MyClass:
    def __init__(self, name):
        self.name = name
```

```python
    def __str__(self):

        return f"MyClass object with name:
{self.name}"


    def __repr__(self):

        return f"MyClass('{self.name}')"


# Usage:

obj = MyClass("John")

print(str(obj))   # Outputs: MyClass object with
name: John

print(repr(obj))  # Outputs: MyClass('John')
```

`__len__`:

The `__len__` method is called by the built-in `len()` function to determine the length of an object.

```python
class MyList:
    def __init__(self, items):
        self.items = items


    def __len__(self):
        return len(self.items)


# Usage:
my_list = MyList([1, 2, 3, 4])
print(len(my_list))  # Outputs: 4
```

`__getitem__` and `__setitem__`:

These methods allow objects to be subscriptable
(support indexing) and mutable.

```python
class MyList:
    def __init__(self, items):
        self.items = items


    def __getitem__(self, index):
```

```
    return self.items[index]


  def __setitem__(self, index, value):

    self.items[index] = value


# Usage:

my_list = MyList([1, 2, 3, 4])

print(my_list[2])   # Outputs: 3

my_list[2] = 99

print(my_list[2])   # Outputs: 99
```

`__call__`:

The `__call__` method allows instances of a class to be called as if they were functions.

```
class MyCallable:

  def __call__(self, x):

    return x * 2


# Usage:

my_callable = MyCallable()
```

```
result = my_callable(3)

print(result)  # Outputs: 6
```

`__add__` and `__sub__`:

These methods define the behavior of the addition and subtraction operators (`+` and `-`).

```python
class MyNumber:
    def __init__(self, value):
        self.value = value

    def __add__(self, other):
        return MyNumber(self.value + other.value)

    def __sub__(self, other):
        return MyNumber(self.value - other.value)

# Usage:
num1 = MyNumber(5)
num2 = MyNumber(3)
result_add = num1 + num2
```

```
result_sub = num1 - num2

print(result_add.value)  # Outputs: 8

print(result_sub.value)  # Outputs: 2
```

These are just a few examples of the many magic methods available in Python. They provide a way to customize and extend the behavior of your classes, making your code more expressive and Pythonic.

Closures and Function Scoping

Closures and function scoping are concepts in Python that are closely related and often used together. Understanding these concepts is essential for writing clean and maintainable code.

Function Scoping:

In Python, a scope is a region of a program where a variable is defined and can be accessed. Python uses a concept called LEGB (Local, Enclosing, Global, Built-in) to determine the scope of a variable.

- Local Scope (L): Variables defined within a function.

- Enclosing Scope (E): Variables in the local scope of enclosing functions (for nested functions).

- Global Scope (G): Variables defined at the top level of a module or explicitly declared as global.

- Built-in Scope (B): Variables that are part of Python's built-in namespace.

Here's an example demonstrating function scoping:

```python
global_variable = "I am global"


def outer_function():
    enclosing_variable = "I am in the enclosing scope"

    def inner_function():
        local_variable = "I am local"
        print(local_variable)
        print(enclosing_variable)
        print(global_variable)
    inner_function()
outer_function()
```

In this example, `local_variable` is in the local scope of `inner_function`, `enclosing_variable` is in the enclosing scope of `inner_function` but local to `outer_function`, and `global_variable` is in the global scope.

Closures:

A closure in Python is a function object that has access to variables in its lexical scope, even when the function is called outside that scope. Closures allow functions to remember the environment in which they were created.

Here's an example of a closure:

```python
def outer_function(x):
    def inner_function(y):
        return x + y
    return inner_function
closure = outer_function(10)
result = closure(5)
print(result)  # Outputs: 15
```

In this example, `outer_function` returns `inner_function`, and the returned function (`closure`) "remembers" the value of `x` from the environment in which it was created. When `closure` is called with `5`, it adds `5` to the remembered value of `x` (`10`), resulting in `15`.

Realworld Example: Function Factory:

Closures are often used to create function factories that generate functions with specific behavior:

```python
def power_function(exponent):
    def power(x):
        return x  exponent
    return power

square = power_function(2)
cube = power_function(3)

print(square(4))  # Outputs: 16
print(cube(3))    # Outputs: 27
```

In this example, `power_function` is a function factory that creates power functions with a specified exponent. The generated functions (`square` and `cube`) remember the exponent value.

Understanding closures and function scoping is crucial for writing modular and reusable code, especially when dealing with higher-order functions and functional programming concepts.

Asynchronous Programming

Asynchronous programming in Python allows you to write concurrent code that can efficiently handle tasks that may block, such as I/O operations, without waiting for each task to complete before moving on to the next one. Asynchronous programming is particularly useful for building responsive and scalable applications.

In Python, there are two main approaches to asynchronous programming: Callbacks and Async/await.

Callbacks:

Callbacks are a traditional way of handling asynchronous operations. Functions take a callback function as an argument, and when the asynchronous operation is complete, the callback function is called.

```
import requests
```

```python
def fetch_data(url, callback):
    response = requests.get(url)
    if response.status_code == 200:
        data = response.json()
        callback(data)
    else:
        callback(None)

def process_data(data):
    if data is not None:
        print("Processing data:", data)
    else:
        print("Error fetching data")

# Usage:
fetch_data("https://jsonplaceholder.typicode.com/todos/1", process_data)
```

Async/Await:

Latest version of Python introduced the `asyncio` module, which provides a native way to write asynchronous code using async/await syntax. Async/await simplifies the syntax and makes asynchronous code more readable.

```python
import asyncio
import aiohttp

async def fetch_data(url):
    async with aiohttp.ClientSession() as session:
        async with session.get(url) as response:
            return await response.json()

async def process_data():
    url = "https://jsonplaceholder.typicode.com/todos/1"
    data = await fetch_data(url)
    if data is not None:
        print("Processing data:", data)
    else:
        print("Error fetching data")
```

```
# Usage:

asyncio.run(process_data())
```

In this example, `asyncio` is used with `aiohttp` to perform an asynchronous HTTP request. The `async def` syntax is used to define asynchronous functions, and `await` is used to call asynchronous functions within other asynchronous functions.

Asyncio Event Loop:

Asyncio uses an event loop to manage asynchronous tasks. The event loop schedules tasks, executes them, and handles I/O operations efficiently.

```python
import asyncio

async def task1():
    print("Task 1 started")
    await asyncio.sleep(2)
    print("Task 1 completed")

async def task2():
    print("Task 2 started")
    await asyncio.sleep(1)
    print("Task 2 completed")

async def main():
    task1_handle = asyncio.create_task(task1())
    task2_handle = asyncio.create_task(task2())

    await task1_handle
    await task2_handle

# Usage:
asyncio.run(main())
```

In this example, `asyncio.create_task` is used to create tasks that run concurrently. The `await` keyword is used to wait for the completion of tasks.

Asynchronous programming in Python is a powerful tool for building scalable and responsive applications. It's particularly beneficial in scenarios where there are many I/O-bound operations that can be executed concurrently.

Multithreading and Multiprocessing

Multithreading and multiprocessing are two approaches to parallelism in Python, allowing you to execute multiple tasks concurrently. These approaches are particularly useful for improving performance in scenarios with CPU-bound or I/O-bound tasks.

Multithreading:

Multithreading involves the execution of multiple threads within the same process. Python's Global Interpreter Lock (GIL) limits the execution of Python bytecode to one thread at a time in a single process. This means that multithreading in Python is often more suitable for I/O-bound tasks rather than CPU-bound tasks.

Here's a simple example using the `threading` module to perform I/O-bound tasks concurrently:

```python
import threading
import requests

def download_page(url):
    response = requests.get(url)
    print(f"Downloaded {len(response.text)} bytes from {url}")

def main():
    urls = ["https://www.example.com",
"https://www.example.org",
"https://www.example.net"]

    # Create and start threads for each URL
    threads = [threading.Thread(target=download_page, args=(url,)) for url in urls]
    for thread in threads:
        thread.start()

    # Wait for all threads to complete
    for thread in threads:
        thread.join()
```

```
if __name__ == "__main__":
    main()
```

Multiprocessing:

Multiprocessing involves the execution of multiple processes, each with its own Python interpreter and memory space.

This approach can take full advantage of multiple CPU cores, making it suitable for CPU-bound tasks. Unlike multithreading, each process in multiprocessing has its own GIL, enabling true parallelism.

Here's an example using the `multiprocessing` module to perform CPU-bound tasks concurrently:

```
import multiprocessing
```

```python
def calculate_square(number):
    result = number * number
    print(f"The square of {number} is {result}")

def main():
    numbers = [1, 2, 3, 4, 5]

    # Create and start processes for each number
    processes = [multiprocessing.Process(target=calculate_square, args=(num,)) for num in numbers]
    for process in processes:
        process.start()

    # Wait for all processes to complete
    for process in processes:
        process.join()

if __name__ == "__main__":
    main()
```

In this example, each process calculates the square of a number independently, taking advantage of multiple CPU cores.

Choosing Between Multithreading and Multiprocessing:

- Use multithreading for I/O-bound tasks, such as network or file I/O, where threads can wait for external operations without blocking the entire process.

- Use multiprocessing for CPU-bound tasks, such as numerical computations, where parallel execution can take full advantage of multiple CPU cores.

It's important to note that due to the GIL in CPython, multithreading may not provide as much performance improvement for CPU-bound tasks as multiprocessing. For CPU-bound tasks, multiprocessing is often a more effective solution.

Regular Expressions

Regular expressions (regex or regexp) are a powerful tool for pattern matching and text manipulation in Python. The `re` module provides support for regular expressions in Python. Regular expressions use a combination of characters and special symbols to define search patterns.

Here's an overview of some commonly used functions and symbols in the `re` module:

Basic Patterns:

- `.` (dot): Matches any character except a newline.

- `^`: Anchors the pattern at the start of the string.

- `$`: Anchors the pattern at the end of the string.

- `[]`: Matches any single character within the brackets.

```
import re

pattern = re.compile(r'^[A-Za-z]+[0-9]*$')

# Check if a string matches the pattern
result = pattern.match("Hello123")
if result:
    print("Match")
else:
    print("No match")
```

Character Classes:

- `\d`: Matches any digit (equivalent to `[0-9]`).

- `\D`: Matches any non-digit.

- `\w`: Matches any word character (alphanumeric + underscore).

- `\W`: Matches any non-word character.

- `\s`: Matches any whitespace character.

- `\S`: Matches any non-whitespace character.

```
pattern = re.compile(r'\d{3}-\d{2}-\d{4}')


# Check if a string matches a Social Security
Number pattern
result = pattern.match("123-45-6789")
if result:
    print("Match")
else:
    print("No match")
```

Quantifiers:

- `*`: Matches 0 or more occurrences of the
preceding character.

- `+`: Matches 1 or more occurrences of the
preceding character.

- `?`: Matches 0 or 1 occurrence of the preceding
character.

- `{n}`: Matches exactly n occurrences of the
preceding character.

- `{n,}` : Matches n or more occurrences of the preceding character.

- `{n,m}` : Matches between n and m occurrences of the preceding character.

```
pattern = re.compile(r'\b\d{3}\b')

# Find all occurrences of three-digit numbers in a string
result = pattern.findall("123 456 789")
print(result)
```

Grouping and Capturing:

Parentheses `()` are used for grouping and capturing portions of the pattern.

```python
pattern = re.compile(r'(\d{3})-(\d{2})-(\d{4})')


# Extract components of a Social Security Number
result = pattern.match("123-45-6789")
if result:
    print("Group 1:", result.group(1))
    print("Group 2:", result.group(2))
    print("Group 3:", result.group(3))
```

Flags:

The `re` module supports flags to modify the behavior of regular expressions. Common flags include `re.IGNORECASE` (ignores case) and `re.MULTILINE` (multiline matching).

```
pattern = re.compile(r'python', re.IGNORECASE)


# Match 'Python', 'PYTHON', etc.

result = pattern.match("Python is powerful")
```

Regular expressions can become quite complex, and mastering them requires practice. The examples provided cover some basics, but there's much more to explore. Regular expressions are widely used for tasks such as data validation, text search and replace, and parsing complex data formats.

Python Standard Library Modules

Python's standard library is a rich collection of modules that provide functionality for various tasks. These modules are part of every Python installation, and they cover a wide range of areas, including file manipulation, networking, data structures, web development, and more. Here are some commonly used Python standard library modules with examples:

1. `os` Module:

The `os` module provides a way of interacting with the operating system. It includes functions to perform tasks such as file and directory manipulation.

```
import os
# Get the current working directory
current_dir = os.getcwd()
print("Current Directory:", current_dir)
```

```python
# List files in the current directory
files = os.listdir(current_dir)
print("Files in Current Directory:", files)
```

2. `datetime` Module:

The `datetime` module provides classes for working with dates and times.

```python
from datetime import datetime, timedelta

# Get the current date and time
now = datetime.now()
print("Current Date and Time:", now)

# Format a date as a string
formatted_date = now.strftime("%Y-%m-%d %H:%M:%S")
print("Formatted Date:", formatted_date)
```

```
# Calculate a future date
future_date = now + timedelta(days=7)
print("Future Date:", future_date)
```

3. `json` Module:

The `json` module provides functions for encoding and decoding JSON data.

```
import json

# Convert a Python dictionary to a JSON string
data = {'name': 'John', 'age': 30, 'city': 'New York'}
json_string = json.dumps(data)
print("JSON String:", json_string)

# Parse a JSON string into a Python object
parsed_data = json.loads(json_string)
print("Parsed Data:", parsed_data)
```

4. `urllib.request` Module:

The `urllib.request` module is used for opening and reading URLs.

```python
from urllib.request import urlopen

# Open and read a URL
response = urlopen('https://www.example.com')
html_content = response.read()
print("HTML Content:", html_content[:100])
```

5. `random` Module:

The `random` module provides functions for generating random numbers.

```python
import random

# Generate a random integer between 1 and 10
random_number = random.randint(1, 10)
print("Random Number:", random_number)
```

```
# Shuffle a list
my_list = [1, 2, 3, 4, 5]
random.shuffle(my_list)
print("Shuffled List:", my_list)
```

6. `re` Module:

The `re` module provides support for regular expressions.

```
import re

# Search for a pattern in a string
pattern = re.compile(r'\b\d{3}\b')
result = pattern.findall("123 456 789")
print("Matches:", result)
```

7. `collections` Module:

The `collections` module provides alternatives to built-in types, such as `Counter` for counting occurrences and `defaultdict` for creating dictionaries with default values.

```
from collections import Counter

# Count occurrences of elements in a list
my_list = ['apple', 'banana', 'apple', 'orange', 'banana', 'apple']
counter = Counter(my_list)
print("Element Counts:", counter)
```

These examples only scratch the surface of the Python standard library. The library is extensive, covering many domains like networking, databases, testing, and more. Before implementing functionality from scratch, it's often worth checking if the standard library provides a suitable module.

The official Python documentation is an excellent

resource for exploring the capabilities of the

standard library: [Python Standard Library

Documentation]

NumPy and SciPy

NumPy and SciPy are two powerful libraries in Python that provide support for numerical and scientific computing. While NumPy focuses on fundamental array operations and mathematical functions, SciPy builds on top of NumPy and provides additional functionality for scientific computing tasks, such as optimization, signal processing, statistics, and more.

NumPy:

NumPy stands for Numerical Python and is the foundational package for numerical computing in Python. It introduces a new data type called `numpy.ndarray` for efficient storage and manipulation of homogeneous data.

```python
# Example 1: Basic NumPy Operations

import numpy as np

# Create a NumPy array
arr = np.array([1, 2, 3, 4, 5])

# Perform basic operations
mean_value = np.mean(arr)
sum_value = np.sum(arr)
max_value = np.max(arr)

print("Array:", arr)
print("Mean:", mean_value)
print("Sum:", sum_value)
print("Max:", max_value)
```

```python
# Example 2: NumPy Arrays and Operations

import numpy as np

# Create NumPy arrays
a = np.array([1, 2, 3])
b = np.array([4, 5, 6])

# Perform array operations
result_addition = a + b
result_multiplication = a * b
result_dot_product = np.dot(a, b)

print("Array A:", a)
print("Array B:", b)
print("Addition:", result_addition)
print("Multiplication:", result_multiplication)
print("Dot Product:", result_dot_product)
```

SciPy:

SciPy builds on NumPy and provides additional functionality for various scientific computing tasks. It includes modules for optimization, signal processing, statistics, integration, interpolation, and more.

```python
# Example: Linear Regression with SciPy

import numpy as np
from scipy.stats import linregress
import matplotlib.pyplot as plt

# Generate sample data
x = np.array([1, 2, 3, 4, 5])
y = np.array([2, 3, 5, 4, 5])

# Perform linear regression
slope, intercept, r_value, p_value, std_err = linregress(x, y)
```

```python
# Plot the data and regression line
plt.scatter(x, y, label='Data Points')
plt.plot(x, slope * x + intercept, color='red', label='Regression Line')
plt.xlabel('X')
plt.ylabel('Y')
plt.legend()
plt.show()

print("Slope:", slope)
print("Intercept:", intercept)
print("R-squared:", r_value2)
```

In this example, SciPy's `linregress` function is used to perform linear regression on a set of data points.

Both NumPy and SciPy are essential tools in the Python ecosystem for numerical and scientific computing. They form the foundation for many other scientific libraries and are widely used in academia and industry for tasks ranging from data analysis to machine learning.

Data Serialization

Data serialization is the process of converting complex data structures or objects into a format that can be easily stored, transmitted, or reconstructed. Serialization is essential for tasks such as saving data to files, sending data over a network, or storing data in databases. In Python, there are several common serialization formats, and two widely used ones are JSON (JavaScript Object Notation) and Pickle.

JSON Serialization:

JSON is a lightweight data interchange format that is easy for humans to read and write. Python provides the `json` module for encoding and decoding JSON data.

Example: Encoding and Decoding JSON

```python
import json

# Python object (dictionary) to be serialized
data = {
    "name": "John",
    "age": 30,
    "city": "New York",
    "is_student": False,
    "grades": [95, 88, 92]
}

# Serialize to JSON (encoding)
json_data = json.dumps(data, indent=2)  # indent for pretty printing
print("Serialized JSON:\n", json_data)

# Deserialize from JSON (decoding)
decoded_data = json.loads(json_data)
print("\nDecoded Data:", decoded_data)
```

In this example, `json.dumps` is used to serialize a Python dictionary to a JSON-formatted string, and `json.loads` is used to deserialize the JSON string back into a Python object.

Pickle Serialization:

Pickle is a Python-specific serialization format that can handle a wider range of Python objects compared to JSON. It is part of the standard library and provides the `pickle` module.

```python
# Example: Pickle Serialization

import pickle

# Python object (list) to be serialized
data = [1, 2, 3, 4, 5]
```

```
# Serialize to Pickle format (encoding)
pickle_data = pickle.dumps(data)
print("Serialized Pickle Data:", pickle_data)

# Deserialize from Pickle format (decoding)
decoded_data = pickle.loads(pickle_data)
print("Decoded Data:", decoded_data)
```

In this example, `pickle.dumps` is used to serialize a Python list to a Pickle-formatted binary string, and `pickle.loads` is used to deserialize the Pickle string back into a Python object.

When to Use JSON vs. Pickle:

- JSON:

  - Human-readable.

  - Interoperable across different programming languages.

- Suitable for simple data structures (dictionaries, lists).

- Pickle:

  - Python-specific format.

  - Can handle a broader range of Python objects, including custom classes.

  - Not secure against arbitrary code execution from untrusted sources.

Additional Notes:

- When working with files, you can use `json.dump` and `json.load` for JSON, and `pickle.dump` and `pickle.load` for Pickle.

- While JSON is commonly used for configuration files and data interchange between different systems, Pickle is more suitable for saving and loading Python-specific objects within the same environment.

Choose the serialization format based on your specific use case, taking into consideration factors such as human-readability, interoperability, and security.

Cython and Numba

Cython and Numba are two tools in the Python ecosystem that aim to improve the performance of Python code by allowing for the incorporation of compiled code or Just-In-Time (JIT) compilation. They are particularly useful for numerical and scientific computing tasks where performance is critical.

Cython:

Cython is a programming language that makes it easy to write C extensions for Python. It allows you to write code with a Python-like syntax and then translate that code into optimized C code that can be compiled and imported as a Python module.

Example: Cythonizing a Python Function

Let's consider a simple Python function that calculates the sum of squares:

```
# pure_python.py
def sum_of_squares(n):
    result = 0
    for i in range(n):
        result += i2
    return result
```

Now, let's create a Cython version of this function:

```
# cython_version.pyx
def sum_of_squares_cython(n):
    result = 0
    for i in range(n):
        result += i2
    return result
```

To use Cython, you need a `setup.py` file to build the extension module:

```python
# setup.py
from setuptools import setup
from Cython.Build import cythonize

setup(
    ext_modules=cythonize("cython_version.pyx")
)
```

After creating these files, you can run the following commands to build the Cython module:

bash

```bash
$ python setup.py build_ext --inplace
```

Now, you can import and use the Cython function in your Python script:

```python
# main.py
from cython_version import sum_of_squares_cython


result = sum_of_squares_cython(10)
print("Sum of squares (Cython):", result)
```

Numba:

Numba is a Just-In-Time (JIT) compiler for Python that translates Python functions into machine code at runtime. It is designed to be easy to use and integrates seamlessly with NumPy.

Example: Numba JIT Compilation

Consider the same sum of squares function. With Numba, you can add a decorator to the Python function to enable JIT compilation:

```python
from numba import jit

@jit(nopython=True)
def sum_of_squares_numba(n):
    result = 0
    for i in range(n):
        result += i2
    return result
```

Now you can use the JIT-compiled function in your script:

```
# main.py

from numba_example import
sum_of_squares_numba


result = sum_of_squares_numba(10)

print("Sum of squares (Numba):", result)
```

Performance Comparison:

To compare the performance of these approaches, you can use the `timeit` module or Jupyter notebooks. In general, the choice between Cython and Numba depends on factors such as ease of use, compatibility with your existing code, and the specific nature of your performance requirements.

Both Cython and Numba can significantly improve the performance of numerical computations, but they have different use cases and trade-offs.

Cython provides a more manual approach, allowing you to mix Python and C code seamlessly, while Numba focuses on automatic JIT compilation, making it simpler to use in many cases.

The optimal choice depends on your specific needs and the nature of your code.

Python Web Frameworks

Python has a vibrant ecosystem of web frameworks that simplify the process of building web applications. These frameworks provide tools, conventions, and abstractions to handle common web development tasks. Here are some popular Python web frameworks with examples:

1. Django:

- Description: Django is a high-level web framework that follows the "batteries-included" philosophy. It provides an ORM, an admin panel, authentication, and many other features out of the box.

- Example:

```python
# models.py
from django.db import models

class Book(models.Model):
    title = models.CharField(max_length=100)
    author = models.CharField(max_length=50)

# views.py
from django.shortcuts import render
from .models import Book

def book_list(request):
    books = Book.objects.all()
    return render(request, 'books/book_list.html', {'books': books})
```

2. Flask:

- Description: Flask is a lightweight and flexible microframework. It provides the essentials for building web applications and leaves many decisions to the developer.

- Example:

```python
from flask import Flask, render_template
app = Flask(__name__)

@app.route('/')
def home():
    return render_template('index.html', title='Home')

if __name__ == '__main__':
    app.run(debug=True)
```

3. FastAPI:

- Description: FastAPI is a modern, fast (high-performance), web framework for building APIs with Python 3.7+ based on standard Python type hints.

- Example:

```python
from fastapi import FastAPI

app = FastAPI()

@app.get("/")
def read_root():
    return {"Hello": "World"}

@app.get("/items/{item_id}")
def read_item(item_id: int, query_param: str = None):
    return {"item_id": item_id, "query_param": query_param}
```

4. Pyramid:

- Description: Pyramid is a flexible and modular web framework. It allows developers to choose the components they want to use and follows the "use what you need" philosophy.

- Example:

```python
from pyramid.config import Configurator
from pyramid.view import view_config

@view_config(route_name='home', renderer='json')
def my_view(request):
    return {'project': 'MyProject'}

if __name__ == '__main__':
    with Configurator() as config:
        config.add_route('home', '/')
        config.scan()
        app = config.make_wsgi_app()
```

```
from wsgiref.simple_server import make_server
server = make_server('0.0.0.0', 6543, app)
server.serve_forever()
```

5. Tornado:

- Description: Tornado is a scalable, non-blocking web server and web application framework. It is designed for handling asynchronous tasks and long-lived connections.

- Example:

```
import tornado.ioloop
import tornado.web

class MainHandler(tornado.web.RequestHandler):
    def get(self):
        self.write("Hello, world")
```

```python
def make_app():
    return tornado.web.Application([
        (r"/", MainHandler),
    ])


if __name__ == "__main__":
    app = make_app()
    app.listen(8888)
    tornado.ioloop.IOLoop.current().start()
```

6. Bottle:

- Description: Bottle is a simple and lightweight micro-framework for small web applications. It is a single-file framework with no external dependencies.

- Example:

```python
from bottle import route, run

@route('/')
def home():
    return "Hello, World!"

if __name__ == '__main__':
    run(host='localhost', port=8080, debug=True)
```

Each web framework has its strengths and use cases, and the choice depends on factors like project requirements, developer preferences, and the desired level of abstraction.

Django is great for full-stack applications, Flask is excellent for microservices, FastAPI is ideal for building APIs, Pyramid offers flexibility, Tornado excels in handling long-lived connections, and Bottle is lightweight and suitable for small projects.

Machine Learning and Data Science Libraries

Python has a rich ecosystem of libraries for machine learning and data science. These libraries provide tools and functions for tasks such as data manipulation, visualization, statistical analysis, machine learning, and deep learning. Here are some prominent libraries along with examples:

1. NumPy:

- Description: NumPy is the fundamental package for scientific computing in Python. It provides support for large, multi-dimensional arrays and matrices, along with mathematical functions to operate on these arrays.

- Example:

```python
import numpy as np

# Create a NumPy array
data = np.array([[1, 2, 3], [4, 5, 6]])

# Perform operations on the array
mean_value = np.mean(data)
sum_value = np.sum(data, axis=1)

print("Array:\n", data)
print("Mean:", mean_value)
print("Sum along axis 1:", sum_value)
```

2. Pandas:

- Description: Pandas is a powerful library for data manipulation and analysis. It provides data structures like DataFrame for efficient handling and manipulation of structured data.

- Example:

```python
import pandas as pd

# Create a Pandas DataFrame
data = {'Name': ['John', 'Alice', 'Bob'],
        'Age': [28, 24, 22],
        'City': ['New York', 'San Francisco', 'Chicago']}

df = pd.DataFrame(data)

# Perform operations on the DataFrame
mean_age = df['Age'].mean()
filtered_data = df[df['Age'] > 25]
```

```
print("DataFrame:\n", df)

print("Mean Age:", mean_age)

print("Filtered Data:\n", filtered_data)
```

3. Matplotlib:

- Description: Matplotlib is a 2D plotting library for creating static, animated, and interactive visualizations in Python.

- Example:

```
import matplotlib.pyplot as plt
import numpy as np

# Generate data
x = np.linspace(0, 2 * np.pi, 100)
y = np.sin(x)

# Create a plot
```

```
plt.plot(x, y, label='sin(x)')

plt.title('Sine Function')

plt.xlabel('x')

plt.ylabel('y')

plt.legend()

plt.show()
```

4. Scikit-learn:

- Description: Scikit-learn is a machine learning library that provides simple and efficient tools for data mining and data analysis. It includes various algorithms for classification, regression, clustering, dimensionality reduction, and more.

- Example:

```
from sklearn.datasets import load_iris
from sklearn.model_selection import train_test_split
```

```python
from sklearn.neighbors import
KNeighborsClassifier

from sklearn.metrics import accuracy_score


# Load the Iris dataset
iris = load_iris()
X, y = iris.data, iris.target


# Split the data into training and testing sets
X_train, X_test, y_train, y_test = train_test_split(X, y,
test_size=0.2, random_state=42)


# Create a k-nearest neighbors classifier
knn = KNeighborsClassifier(n_neighbors=3)


# Train the classifier
knn.fit(X_train, y_train)


# Make predictions on the test set
y_pred = knn.predict(X_test)


# Evaluate accuracy
```

```
accuracy = accuracy_score(y_test, y_pred)
print("Accuracy:", accuracy)
```

5. TensorFlow:

- Description: TensorFlow is an open-source machine learning library developed by Google. It provides a comprehensive set of tools for building and deploying machine learning models, especially for deep learning.

- Example:

```
import tensorflow as tf
from tensorflow.keras import layers, models

# Create a simple neural network model
model = models.Sequential([
    layers.Flatten(input_shape=(28, 28)),    # Flatten the input
```

```python
    layers.Dense(128, activation='relu'),    # Fully
connected layer with ReLU activation

    layers.Dropout(0.2),                # Dropout layer
for regularization

    layers.Dense(10, activation='softmax')   #
Output layer with softmax activation

])


# Compile the model

model.compile(optimizer='adam',

        loss='sparse_categorical_crossentropy',

        metrics=['accuracy'])


# Print model summary

model.summary()
```

6. PyTorch:

- Description: PyTorch is an open-source machine
learning library developed by Facebook. It is known

for its dynamic computational graph and is widely used for deep learning tasks.

- Example:

```
import torch
import torch.nn as nn


# Create a simple neural network model
class SimpleNet(nn.Module):
    def __init__(self):
        super(SimpleNet, self).__init__()
        self.flatten = nn.Flatten()
        self.fc = nn.Linear(28 * 28, 10)

    def forward(self, x):
        x = self.flatten(x)
        x = self.fc(x)
        return x


# Instantiate the model
```

```
model = SimpleNet()

# Print model architecture
print(model)
```

These libraries form the foundation of Python's
ecosystem for machine learning and data science.
Depending on your specific tasks and
requirements, you may choose a combination of
these libraries to perform data analysis,
visualization, and machine learning.

GUI Development

Python offers several libraries for developing graphical user interfaces (GUIs), making it easy to create desktop applications with graphical interfaces. Here are some popular Python GUI libraries with examples:

1. Tkinter:

- Description: Tkinter is the standard GUI toolkit included with Python. It is simple, easy to use, and provides a wide range of GUI components.

- Example: Hello World with Tkinter:

```python
import tkinter as tk

def say_hello():
    label.config(text="Hello, " + entry.get())
```

```python
# Create the main window
root = tk.Tk()
root.title("Hello Tkinter")

# Create and pack widgets
label = tk.Label(root, text="Enter your name:")
label.pack()

entry = tk.Entry(root)
entry.pack()

button = tk.Button(root, text="Say Hello",
command=say_hello)
button.pack()

# Start the Tkinter event loop
root.mainloop()
```

2. PyQt:

- Description: PyQt is a set of Python bindings for Qt libraries. It is powerful and provides a wide range of features for building modern and feature-rich applications.

- Example: Hello World with PyQt:

```python
from PyQt5.QtWidgets import QApplication,
QLabel, QWidget, QVBoxLayout, QPushButton


def say_hello():
    label.setText("Hello, " + entry.text())


# Create the application and main window
app = QApplication([])
window = QWidget()
window.setWindowTitle("Hello PyQt")


# Create widgets and layout
```

```python
label = QLabel("Enter your name:")
entry = QLineEdit()
button = QPushButton("Say Hello")
button.clicked.connect(say_hello)

layout = QVBoxLayout()
layout.addWidget(label)
layout.addWidget(entry)
layout.addWidget(button)

window.setLayout(layout)

# Show the window
window.show()

# Run the application
app.exec_()
```

3. Kivy:

- Description: Kivy is an open-source Python framework for developing multi-touch applications. It is well-suited for applications targeting multiple platforms, including mobile devices.

- Example: Hello World with Kivy:

```
from kivy.app import App
from kivy.uix.label import Label
from kivy.uix.button import Button
from kivy.uix.boxlayout import BoxLayout
from kivy.uix.textinput import TextInput


class HelloWorldApp(App):
    def build(self):
        layout = BoxLayout(orientation='vertical')

        label = Label(text='Enter your name:')
        entry = TextInput()
```

```python
        button = Button(text='Say Hello',
on_press=self.say_hello)

        layout.add_widget(label)

        layout.add_widget(entry)

        layout.add_widget(button)


        return layout


    def say_hello(self, instance):
        label.text = 'Hello, ' + entry.text


if __name__ == '__main__':
    HelloWorldApp().run()
```

4. wxPython:

- Description: wxPython is a set of Python bindings for the wxWidgets library. It provides native-looking widgets on various platforms and is suitable for creating desktop applications.

- Example: Hello World with wxPython:

```python
import wx


class HelloWorldApp(wx.Frame):
    def __init__(self, *args, kw):
        super(HelloWorldApp, self).__init__(*args, kw)


        panel = wx.Panel(self)
        sizer = wx.BoxSizer(wx.VERTICAL)


        label = wx.StaticText(panel, label='Enter your name:')
        entry = wx.TextCtrl(panel)
        button = wx.Button(panel, label='Say Hello')
        button.Bind(wx.EVT_BUTTON, self.say_hello)


        sizer.Add(label, 0, wx.ALL, 5)
        sizer.Add(entry, 0, wx.ALL, 5)
        sizer.Add(button, 0, wx.ALL, 5)
```

```python
        panel.SetSizer(sizer)
        self.Show()


    def say_hello(self, event):
        label.SetLabel('Hello, ' + entry.GetValue())


if __name__ == '__main__':
    app = wx.App(False)
    frame = HelloWorldApp(None, title='Hello wxPython')
    app.MainLoop()
```

These examples demonstrate how to create simple GUI applications using different Python GUI libraries. The choice of library depends on factors such as ease of use, platform compatibility, and the specific requirements of your application. Each library provides a set of tools for building user interfaces, and you can choose the one that best fits your needs.

Custom Module and Package Development

In Python, a module is a file containing Python definitions and statements. A package is a way of organizing related modules into a single directory hierarchy. Let's explore how to create custom modules and packages with examples:

Custom Module:

To create a custom module, you need to save Python code in a separate file with a `.py` extension. Let's create a simple module named `math_operations.py` that contains basic mathematical operations:

```python
# math_operations.py


def add(x, y):
    return x + y


def subtract(x, y):
    return x - y


def multiply(x, y):
    return x * y


def divide(x, y):
    if y == 0:
        return "Cannot divide by zero"
    return x / y
```

Now, you can use this module in another Python script by importing it:

```
# main.py

import math_operations

result_add = math_operations.add(5, 3)
result_subtract = math_operations.subtract(8, 4)

print("Addition:", result_add)
print("Subtraction:", result_subtract)
```

Custom Package:

A package is a way to organize multiple modules into a single directory. To create a package, you need to have a directory containing an `__init__.py` file (which can be empty) and multiple Python modules.

Let's create a package named `shapes` with two modules, `circle.py` and `rectangle.py`:

shapes/

|-- __init__.py

|-- circle.py

|-- rectangle.py

Contents of `circle.py`:

shapes/circle.py

```
import math

def area(radius):
    return math.pi * radius2

def circumference(radius):
    return 2 * math.pi * radius
```

Contents of `rectangle.py`:

```
# shapes/rectangle.py


def area(length, width):
    return length * width


def perimeter(length, width):
    return 2 * (length + width)
```

Contents of `__init__.py` (can be empty):

shapes/__init__.py

Now, you can use the package and its modules in another Python script:

```
# main.py


from shapes import circle, rectangle


radius = 5
```

```
length = 4
width = 3


circle_area = circle.area(radius)
rectangle_area = rectangle.area(length, width)


print("Circle Area:", circle_area)
print("Rectangle Area:", rectangle_area)
```

In this example, `shapes` is a package, and `circle` and `rectangle` are modules within that package.

To summarize, creating a custom module involves saving Python code in a separate file, and creating a custom package involves organizing related modules into a directory with an `__init__.py` file. Once created, you can use `import` statements to access the functionalities defined in modules and packages from other Python scripts.

Debugging and Profiling

Debugging and profiling are essential aspects of software development. Python provides tools for debugging and profiling to help identify and fix issues in your code. Here, I'll explain how to use the built-in `pdb` debugger for debugging and the `cProfile` module for profiling.

Debugging with `pdb`:

The `pdb` module is a built-in Python debugger that allows you to interactively debug your code. You can set breakpoints, inspect variables, and step through the code.

Example:

Consider the following simple script:

```python
# debug_example.py

def divide(x, y):
    result = x / y
    return result

def main():
    a = 10
    b = 2
    result = divide(a, b)
    print("Result:", result)

if __name__ == "__main__":
    main()
```

To debug this script using `pdb`, insert the following line where you want to set a breakpoint:

```
import pdb; pdb.set_trace()
```

For example:

```python
# debug_example.py


def divide(x, y):
    import pdb; pdb.set_trace()
    result = x / y
    return result


def main():
    a = 10
    b = 2
    result = divide(a, b)
    print("Result:", result)


if __name__ == "__main__":
    main()
```

When you run the script, it will stop at the breakpoint, and you can use various commands such as `n` (next), `c` (continue), `p` (print), and others to navigate and inspect the code.

Profiling with `cProfile`:

The `cProfile` module provides a way to profile Python programs for performance analysis. It records the time spent in each function and helps identify bottlenecks.

Example:

Consider the following script:

```
# profile_example.py

def slow_function():
    import time
    time.sleep(2)
```

```python
def main():
    for _ in range(5):
        slow_function()

if __name__ == "__main__":
    main()
```

To profile this script using `cProfile`, you can run it from the command line:

```bash
python -m cProfile profile_example.py
```

This will print a detailed profiling report, showing the time spent in each function.

You can also use `cProfile` programmatically in your script:

```python
# profile_example.py

import cProfile

def slow_function():
    import time
    time.sleep(2)

def main():
    for _ in range(5):
        slow_function()

if __name__ == "__main__":
    cProfile.run("main()", sort="cumulative")
```

This will produce a similar profiling report but within the script.

These are basic examples, and both debugging and profiling can be more complex for larger projects. However, using `pdb` for debugging and `cProfile` for profiling provides a good starting point for identifying and addressing issues in your Python code.